Emma S. Reid

The Money Mindful Millennial

A Practical Guide to Saving Smart and Spending Intentionally

By Emma S. Reid

Emma S. Reid

ISBN: 978-1-965289-09-9

Table of Contents

Emma S. Reid

Introduction: The Why Behind This Book

I wrote *The Money Mindful Millennial* because I've lived and am currently living this journey.

Like probably many of you, I didn't grow up with a financial playbook. I wasn't handed a manual on how to budget, save, or navigate the real cost of adulthood. What I did have was responsibility, a lot of it, and the relentless pressure to figure it all out.

Over time, I discovered something powerful: when you pair intentionality with information, everything changes. Budgeting doesn't have to feel like a punishment. Bulk buying isn't about hoarding: it's about strategy. Planning ahead doesn't mean you can't be spontaneous: it just means you're choosing your moments with clarity.

This book is the guide I wish I had in my twenties. It's the advice I now live by in my thirties, and the kind of real-talk I share with friends, coworkers, and anyone who's ever said, "I just want to be smarter with money." It's practical. It's judgment-free. And most importantly, it's rooted in the real life of a millennial juggling work, family, culture, and the chaos in between.

We, the millennials, were born between roughly 1981 and 1996. We've seen it all. We grew up with landlines and AIM, then adapted to smartphones and social media. We watched 9/11 unfold on TV in real-time, graduated into a recession, and now raise kids in a world where eggs cost more than our childhood lunches (please check those egg cartons before purchasing for broken eggs, please). And many of us are first-generation Americans, balancing tradition with assimilation, expectations with reality. And while the internet and AI can teach you how to do just about anything, it rarely hands you the tools to build financial confidence, especially if you didn't grow up with it.

I didn't come from money. I wasn't taught how to save or spend responsibly. I learned through trial, error, and a lot of humbling moments. And while this book isn't filled with investment advice, tax strategies, or arguments about renting vs. buying — because I'm not a licensed financial advisor — it **is** filled with the lessons that have helped me create a life that reflects my values.

This is for the parents buying diapers on a budget. The folks eyeing a vacation but unsure how to afford it without guilt. The planners, the side hustlers, the coupon clippers, and people who just want to do better, or learn how to.

I'm a mom of two young boys, a wife, and the eldest of three siblings. As the oldest daughter, I've naturally taken on the role of family manager — the one everyone turns to for advice, planning, and support. Over the years, that role has given me a front-row seat to the real-life challenges people face when it comes to money. It's also made me my family's go-to source for budgeting tips, thoughtful planning, and creative problem-solving. So I figured, why not write it all down? Why not channel the advice I give every day into something that can help more people feel confident and in control of their financial lives?

Whether you're here to overhaul your budget, get better with groceries, or just feel a little less alone in your financial journey, I'm glad you're here. Let's take the overwhelm out of money and bring the mindfulness in.

Let's get into it.

Emma S. Reid

Chapter 1: Budgeting Without Burnout

Traditional budgets often feel like crash diets: rigid, guilt-inducing, and hard to stick to. That's because they usually focus on restriction instead of intention and practicality. They tell you what you *can't* do rather than helping you say yes to what matters most or giving you the flexibility to. But what if your budget could reflect your values instead of your vices? What if it helped you build a life you actually want to live?

What Is a Values-Based Budget?

A values-based budget starts with *you*. Your lifestyle, your goals, your priorities. Whether it's organic groceries, weekend getaways with your kids, time to create, or giving back to your community, your budget should make room for what lights you up. It's not just about cutting back; it's about investing in the life you care about.

The beauty of this approach is that it reframes budgeting from being a tool of restriction to a tool of alignment. You're not depriving yourself, you're choosing with purpose.

Step One: Get Clear on Your Current Spending

You can't make a map without knowing where you are. Before you can create a values-aligned budget, you need a clear picture of your current spending habits. This doesn't need to be overwhelming.

Here's how to start:

- **Pull up your last 1–3 months of bank or credit card statements.** Look for patterns—categories where your money naturally flows (like dining out, subscriptions, kids' activities, travel, etc.).

- **Use a digital budgeting tool.** If you're comfortable with apps, services like Plaid (not sponsored) can link your accounts and automatically categorize your spending, saving you time.

- **Go old-school if you prefer.** Download your statements and use a spreadsheet or even colored highlighters to group similar expenses together.

You're not judging or changing anything yet. You're just observing. Think of it as data gathering, not discipline.

Step Two: Identify What Actually Matters

Once you know where your money is going, take a step back and ask:

- What expenses bring me the most joy or peace of mind?

- Which ones support my values (health, family, freedom, creativity)?

- What feels wasteful, stressful, or simply misaligned with the life I want?

You might find that the $5 coffee actually *is* worth it because it gives you a moment of calm before a busy day. But maybe the $50 subscription you forgot to cancel isn't.

Your values will be your compass. Use them to reallocate, not just cut, so your money supports your goals, not someone else's advertising.

We will talk more about daily coffees, subscriptions, and credit cards later in this book.

Step Three: Start Building the Budget

Once you've defined what matters and what doesn't, you can start sketching out a realistic, flexible budget around:

- **Essential expenses** (housing, groceries, childcare, insurance)

- **Value-based priorities** (travel, creative time, weekend fun)

- **Financial goals** (savings, debt payoff, investing)

- **Non-essentials to reduce or cut** (impulse buys, unused or minimally used services, unused credit cards with fees)

This doesn't have to be perfect. It's a living plan. Give yourself grace. The goal is to *support your values without burning out* financially, emotionally, or mentally.

Exercise

To help support this exercise, see the **Values Discovery Worksheet** & **Sample Monthly Budget Template (Values-Based)** in the Appendix Sections 1.1 and 1.2.

Emma S. Reid

Chapter 2: Get the Deal, Keep the Quality

Being financially mindful doesn't mean living a life of restriction. It means getting creative and intentional about how you spend. There are ways to enjoy the things you love **without paying full price**, and this Chapter is all about that. Whether it's your weekly groceries, a family vacation, or upgrading your wardrobe: **you can keep the quality and still get the deal**.

Tech Tools That Save You Money

Here are a few simple tools that can help you save money **without clipping coupons** (not sponsored):

- **Rakuten** (formerly Ebates): Earn cash back at stores you already shop at—just activate the extension and shop as usual.

- **Honey**: Automatically finds and applies promo codes at checkout. It also has a rewards system (Honey Gold) that can convert into gift cards.

- **Ibotta**: Especially useful for groceries, Ibotta gives you cash back for scanning receipts or shopping through the app.

These apps take just a few minutes to set up and can save you hundreds over time with minimal effort.

You might consider exploring your local grocery store and if they have an app that allows you to clip virtual coupons.

Credit Cards: Friend or Foe?

If you use credit cards, you can absolutely make them work in your favor, but only if you follow two key rules:

1. **Pay them off in full each month.**
   Otherwise, the interest you'll pay wipes out any rewards you earn.

2. **Know your perks, and use them.**
   Many premium cards charge annual fees that range from $95 to $695. If you're going to pay that, make sure you're taking full advantage. Some cards offer perks like:

   ○ Free TSA PreCheck or Global Entry

   ○ Statement credits for dining, rideshares, or streaming

   ○ Travel insurance and car rental coverage

   ○ Lounge access during travel (a sanity and money-saver if you fly often)

   ○ Bonus points on categories like groceries, gas, or travel

   ○ Partner deals on rideshare or food delivery services

If you aren't using the benefits, consider switching to a no-fee card that better fits your lifestyle. The goal is to **make the card work for you**, not the other way around.

Free and Low-Cost Treasures

Before you buy something new, check if you can get it **for free or for less**:

- **Buy Nothing Groups**: Local Facebook-based communities where neighbors give away items they no longer need, from toys to furniture to unopened food.

- **Facebook Marketplace**: A goldmine for quality secondhand goods. Filter by location, price, and category to find deals near you. I've purchased a lot of educational toys from here, like Montessori-type puzzles!

- **Nextdoor and Craigslist**: Also good options, especially for furniture or home goods.

Buying second-hand is not only more affordable, it's also more sustainable. Win-win.

Exercise

To help support this exercise, see the **Deal Tracker Worksheet** in the Appendix Section 2.1.

Chapter 3: Your Daily Cost Factor — What Are Your Habits Costing You?

What *Is* Your Daily Cost Factor?

The Daily Cost Factor is the idea that **small, daily purchases**—think coffee, lunch, impulse snacks, beauty routines—can silently drain your finances over time.

Let's do the math on a few typical habits:

Habit	D	M	Y
Coffee + muffin	$7	$210	$2,555
Lunch out	$12	$360	$4,380

Nails every 2 weeks	—	$100	$1,200

That's over **$8,600 a year**, without even touching clothing, rideshare, or random Target runs.

This Isn't About Guilt

This isn't about making you feel bad or asking you to give up joy. It's about **awareness** and **intentionality**.

If your $5 latte is your favorite moment of peace each day, great. But own that decision, and make sure it fits within your values-based budget.

What this teaches us is that **money leaks in tiny, quiet ways**, and if we can plug those leaks, we unlock real freedom.

Why It Matters: Compounding Over Time

Let's say you cut out $10 of unnecessary spending a day and redirect it into a high-yield savings account or investment:

- $10/day = $3,650/year

- Invested at 7% over 10 years = ~**$51,000+**

How to Track Your Own Daily Cost Factor

Ask yourself:

- What are 3 "daily habits" I spend on without thinking?

- How often do I eat out or order in each week?

- Do I subscribe to things I forgot about?

(You'll be surprised by what you uncover.)

Credit Card Cleanup

This is the perfect moment to also **do a credit card inventory**:

- List every card you own

- Note the balance, annual fee, and benefit (if any)

- Ask: **Do I actually use this?**

- Cancel what you don't need (especially if you're not paying it off monthly)

The more cards you have floating around, the easier it is to forget a due date, get hit with interest, or worse, damage your credit score.

Where to Redirect Those Savings

Instead of letting your money disappear into lattes and late-night Amazon scrolls, what could you do?

- Start or grow an **emergency fund**
- Book a vacation you've been dreaming about
- Make a real dent in **debt**
- Invest in yourself (education, coaching, etc.)

Exercise

To help support this exercise, see the **Daily Cost Factor and Credit Card Clean Up Worksheets** in the Appendix Section 3.1 & 3.2.

Chapter 4: Money-Smart Motherhood

Becoming a mom changed everything for me, and especially how I think about money. Suddenly, saving wasn't just a nice-to-have; it became a necessity. The good news? Motherhood communities and a little creativity can turn saving and spending less into a fun and rewarding adventure.

This Chapter is the longest, partly because I have a lot of thoughts on the topic, and partly because I wanted to consolidate as much as I could in one place, knowing it may not apply to everyone reading this book.

Newborns & the Hospital Hustle

When you're recovering from birth and caring for a tiny human, saving money might not be top of mind, but trust me, those early decisions can set the tone for budget-smart parenting. One of the best tips I ever received (and now pass on to every new mom I know): **take *everything* the hospital gives you.** I mean it. If it's in your room and it's been opened, it's yours.

That half-used bottle of baby soap? Grab it. The stack of newborn diapers in the bassinet drawer? Into the bag. The mesh underwear, jumbo pads, peri bottle, witch hazel pads, and cooling spray for postpartum healing? Yours. They can't use them for someone else, and if you leave it behind, it'll go straight into the trash. You're not being greedy, you're being smart and diverting it from going to a landfill. Most hospitals will even send you with a goodie bag.

And let's talk about those iconic hospital baby blankets. You know the white ones with the pink and blue stripes? Are they fancy? No. Are they magical? Also no. But they're absorbent, soft (kinda), and *perfect* for swaddling, spit-up, makeshift burp cloths, and even baby towels when you get home from the hospital. They're workhorses in disguise, and you'll thank yourself for grabbing a couple on your way out. (Bonus points if you ask the nurse for extras before discharge, as most are more than happy to oblige.)

Quick Tip: Bring an extra tote bag in your hospital bag just for this purpose.

It's not about being cheap, it's about realizing that every small cost avoided adds up. Parenthood is full of expenses you can't control, but this? This one you can.

Newborn Clothes: Cute, But Caution

Newborn clothes are *adorable*, and people *love* to gift them. But here's the thing: your baby might only wear that "0–3 months" onesie once (or not at all) before outgrowing it. One of the best pieces of advice I got as a new mom? **Don't rip off the tags or wash everything at once.**

Wash a handful of the essentials: zip-up sleepers, a few soft onesies, and some footed pants, then set the rest aside. Babies grow fast, and depending on their size at birth, they may skip straight to 3–6 months. If you hold off, you can either:

- **Exchange** some of the new-with-tags clothes for larger sizes or **store credit** (or better yet — diapers!),

- **Regift** them to someone else (just keep track of who gave what), or

- **Donate** them to a local shelter or mom-to-mom group that can use them.

Less waste, less clutter, and more flexibility, because the last thing you need is a dresser full of unused newborn outfits when what you *really* need is more burp cloths and wipes.

Breast Pump & Supplies

One of the most overlooked freebies in new motherhood? **Your insurance-covered breast pump.** Yes, *most insurance plans* will fully cover a pump for **every single pregnancy.** That includes electric models, manuals, and in many cases, **a starter set of milk storage bags**.

Before you buy anything out-of-pocket, check your coverage (there are even services that handle the process for you and some OB offices will guide you too). The pump you receive might not be the fanciest or hands-free, but don't underestimate it! **Try the free one first** before spending $300+ on an upgrade you may not need, like, or use.

And when it comes to accessories, hold off on buying dozens of extra parts, flanges, or bags. Use the basics first. Once you get into a routine (or if you decide to combo feed or switch to formula), you'll have a clearer idea of what's worth investing in, and what's just clutter.

Bonus tip: Some FSA/HSA funds can also be used for pump parts, lactation support, and storage bags: don't leave money on the table.

Maternity Clothes: The Biggest Waste of Money (My Personal Opinion)

Maternity clothes can quickly become one of the biggest expenses during pregnancy, but are they really necessary? While some jobs or special events might require you to purchase new or specific attire, many moms-to-be don't actually need to buy a whole new wardrobe.

For the first few months, your regular clothes will likely still fit or can be layered and stretched to accommodate your growing belly. And honestly, is anyone going to judge a pregnant woman for wearing the same comfortable outfits repeatedly? Probably not.

If you do feel the need to purchase maternity-specific pieces, consider alternatives like renting or purchasing second-hand. Renting lets you wear what you need without the burden of keeping a new wardrobe after birth. Plus, second hand maternity clothes are a great budget-friendly option and much more sustainable.

If you do purchase maternity clothes new, plan ahead to resell them afterward or give them to a friend. This way, you can recoup some of your investment instead of letting those items sit unused in your closet or give them a second life.

In short, before splurging on maternity wear, take a step back, get creative with what you already own, and explore renting or buying second hand. Your wallet will thank you, and so will the planet. I bought a full-priced sweater dress that I wore exactly once, for a work event during my second pregnancy, and I still regret it to this day.

Rethinking the Nursery: Function Over Flex

There's a spending trap I see *all the time*, and it starts with the nursery. A brand-new baby is arriving, and suddenly there's this pressure to create the perfect Pinterest-worthy room: matching furniture sets, top-of-the-line wallpaper, in-season decor from Pottery Barn. And listen, I get it, the excitement is real. But let's be honest: your newborn will not remember where their dresser came from or whether their rocking chair was trending on social media.

So here's my advice: skip the showroom nursery. You'll save hundreds (sometimes thousands), and your baby will be just as loved, cozy, and safe.

Buy second-hand whenever you can. The only items I recommend buying brand-new are the crib and mattress — for safety reasons. But if you know someone who's passing theirs along and it meets current safety standards, even better.

For our first child, we turned a spare room into the nursery. We weren't hosting anyone at the time, so we used the existing dresser from our guest room that also doubled as a changing table. My husband built the crib, and we brought in our spare couch for those long nights. I did buy a new nursing chair, and I don't regret it. I knew I'd spend a lot of hours in it, so I made comfort a priority there.

By the time we had our second child, we had even less space and even more perspective. We decided to stay in our modest home instead of upgrading to a larger one, which meant we had to get creative. I cleaned out a closet that had an old plastic dresser from Target and used it to store the 0–3 month clothes and accessories. I moved the nursing chair into our bedroom and used baskets to organize things like burp cloths, diapers, and swaddles. I bought *nothing* new to set up his space. When he turned 3 months, we rotated him into the nursery and moved our toddler into what was once the guest room.

And for a special touch, I painted custom nursery art for each of the boys — something unique made by their mom. You don't have to be an artist to create something special. If painting isn't your thing, another great budget-friendly option is to buy printable artwork from Etsy and frame it yourself. It's personal, beautiful, and a fraction of the cost of store-bought decor.

The lesson? Babies need love, routine, and safe sleep, not designer furniture that they will outgrow. Resist the pressure to overspend on aesthetics that serve other people's expectations more than your family's actual needs. Be thoughtful about what matters to *you*, and give yourself permission to repurpose, borrow, and simplify.

Where Kids Eat Free

Feeding the family can be a big budget line item, but many restaurants offer "Kids Eat Free" nights or special deals. For example, some chains have dedicated days (like Tuesday nights) when kids can eat for free with a paying adult. It's a smart way to enjoy a night out without the usual stress on your wallet.

Free and Low-Cost Family Fun

Don't underestimate the power of local museums, parks, and libraries, where many offer free family nights or special programming. Our local museum hosts free family nights every Thursday, and it's a highlight of our week. These outings offer quality time and entertainment without breaking the bank.

Second-Hand Clothes: A Mom's Secret Weapon

I'll admit, I don't buy new clothes for my boys anymore, especially because daycare is a mess magnet! Between food spills, paint, and all the other daily adventures, second-hand clothes are just smarter. They also grow out of everything so fast.

For holidays or themed school days, I head to local thrift stores. Take the 12 Days of Christmas theme for example, who has the time or budget to keep up? I can find costumes or themed pajamas at a steep discount, and since my kids will only wear them once, why pay full price?

Tiny Libraries, Big Wins: Free Books & Family Adventures

One of my favorite budget-friendly mom hacks? The Little Free Libraries that are popping up in neighborhoods everywhere.

As a family, we love taking walks to explore different Little Free Libraries near us. We bring a book or two we've already read and trade them for something new. It's a fun mini-adventure, totally free, and teaches kids the joy of sharing, reading, and reusing.

These tiny libraries are more than just a cute idea, they're a smart, sustainable way to build your family's book collection, encourage literacy, and give books a second (or third) life.

So next time your toddler is bouncing off the walls, try this: grab a few books, find a Little Free Library nearby, and make it a walk-and-swap kind of outing. You'll save money, create a meaningful family ritual, and maybe even find your next favorite bedtime story.

To learn more about the Little Free Library, visit: https://littlefreelibrary.org/

Tips for Money-Smart Moms:

- Join local Buy Nothing or moms' swap groups on Facebook or Nextdoor.

- Keep an eye out for "Kids Eat Free" nights at your favorite restaurants.

- Explore your local library and museums for free or discounted family events.

- Shop second-hand for nursery items, everyday clothes, and holiday costumes.

Exercise

To help support this exercise, see the **Kids Eat Free Weekly Schedule Worksheet** in the Appendix Section 4.1.

Emma S. Reid

Chapter 5: Health Insurance Hacks & Medical Bill Mastery

Medical bills can be confusing, stressful, and, if you're not careful, costly. But understanding how your insurance works and mastering your medical bills can save you hundreds, even thousands, of dollars. Here's how to take control.

Know Your Key Terms: Deductible, Out-of-Pocket Max, and Copays

Before you even see a doctor, get clear on your health plan's deductible which is the amount you pay before the full benefits of your insurance kicks in, and your out-of-pocket maximum which is the total amount you'll pay in a year before insurance covers 100%. Also, know your copays, the fixed amount you pay for doctor visits or prescriptions. These numbers are the foundation for budgeting healthcare costs.

Preventative Care vs. Specialized Care: What's Covered?

Most insurance plans cover preventative care like annual physicals, vaccines, and screenings at 100%. Specialized care or treatments for ongoing conditions often involve copays or coinsurance. Knowing which services fall into which category can help you avoid surprise bills.

Telehealth and Virtual Care: A Lower-Cost Alternative

Did you know many minor illnesses or routine consultations can be handled through telehealth services? Virtual visits typically cost less than in-person appointments and often have lower copays. They're especially useful for colds, flu, allergies, or medication refills. Check if your insurance plan covers telehealth and consider it as a first step for non-emergency care. Not only can this save money, but it also saves time.

Always Request Itemized Bills

Here's a golden rule: **never** assume a medical bill is accurate. Always ask for an itemized bill and compare it to your Explanation of Benefits (EOB) from your insurer. Errors happen, like duplicate charges, services you didn't receive, or out-of-network fees that shouldn't apply. Catching these errors can save you big.

How to Appeal Inaccurate Charges

If you find a mistake, don't hesitate to dispute it. Contact your provider's billing department and your insurance company. Many providers actually outsource their billing and I have had to forward receipts of payment from in-office visits on some occasions (which is insane to me). Be persistent and keep records of all communications.

I once overpaid $700 due to a billing error. I only discovered it two years later after carefully reviewing my bills and EOBs. Frustratingly, no one at the billing office volunteered to refund me and I had to follow up multiple times before they sent a check. That $700 could have gone toward a vacation, debt payoff, or investments.

Make the Most of FSA/HSA Accounts

Flexible Spending Accounts (FSA) and Health Savings Accounts (HSA) let you set aside pre-tax dollars for medical expenses, reducing your taxable income. HSAs, in particular, are powerful because funds roll over year to year and can be invested. Use these accounts for copays, prescriptions, and even some over-the-counter items. FSAs are a little more restrictive on what you can use them for (before you meet your deductible) and they must be used within the calendar year versus rolling over like an HSA.

Pro Tips:

- Track how much you've paid toward your deductible throughout the year. When a doctor's office quotes a charge, tell them when you've met your deductible and ask them to re-verify your balance with your insurance before paying upfront.

- If you pay upfront, follow up to request a refund for any overpayment once your insurer processes the claim.

- Keep organized records of all medical bills, EOBs, and communications. This saves time and stress during disputes.

- Explore telehealth options covered by your insurance to save money on minor illnesses and routine visits.

Emma S. Reid

Chapter 6: Food Budgeting Without Sacrificing Taste

Feeding yourself and your family well doesn't mean breaking the bank or eating bland meals. With a little planning and some smart shopping hacks, you can enjoy delicious food while keeping your budget intact.

Meal Planning and Batch Cooking

One of the easiest ways to save money on food is to plan your meals in advance. And batch cooking allows you to prepare larger quantities of meals, then refrigerate or freeze portions for later. This not only saves time on busy days but helps prevent last-minute takeout splurges.

Budget Grocery Stores and Price Matching

Learn your local stores that offer the best deals. Budget-friendly grocery stores often have staples at lower prices without sacrificing quality. Many chains also offer price matching where you can bring a competitor's ad, and they'll match the lower price. This can be a game-changer if you're strategic about where and when you shop.

Loyalty Apps for Free Meals and Discounts

Grocery store apps often have exclusive coupons, deals, and even free items for loyal customers. Signing up for loyalty programs can lead to serious savings over time. Don't forget to check app notifications or weekly emails for extra discounts.

The Freezer and Pantry Challenge

One month, I challenged myself to "shop" my pantry and freezer before heading to the store. By planning meals around what I already had on hand, and buying only what I needed, I saved $200! Pairing this with coupons and store loyalty points, my food budget started working for me, not against me.

Seasonal Deals on Fruits and Vegetables

I always keep an eye out for steep discounts on fruit and vegetables. When I find a good deal, I buy extra, prep it immediately, and freeze it for future meals and snacks. This approach keeps healthy options in the freezer year-round and saves money. Also a great hack for making smoothies!

Exercise

To help support this exercise, see the **Pantry Inventory Tracker Worksheet** in the Appendix Section 5.1.

Emma S. Reid

Chapter 7: Travel Without the Debt Spiral

Travel hacking isn't a myth, you just need to be strategic about how you earn and spend points, pick your timing, and plan smart.

Please, I beg you—avoid budget airlines. We're past that age where saving $40 on a ticket is worth risking delayed or canceled flights. And book direct flights when possible. It's often worth the slightly higher cost for peace of mind and a smoother trip.

Credit Card Point Hacking

Use credit cards that reward everyday purchases with travel points. I personally buy airfare with my points-earning card, then use those points for nicer hotel stays. Just remember the golden rules: always pay your balance off in full and know the fees before you commit.

Off-Peak and Shoulder-Season Travel

Flying and lodging costs drop by 30–50% during off-peak or shoulder seasons. Setting price alerts on apps like Google Flights or Hopper can help you snag the best deals. Traveling during these times means fewer crowds and often a more relaxed experience, too.

Affordable Family Trips and Road Trips

Family vacations don't have to cost a fortune. Consider road trips or nearby destinations where you can cut down on airfare and hotel costs. Pack meals and snacks for the road to save on dining out.

Chapter 8: Mindset, Minimalism, and Money

Some of the most powerful savings come not from how you spend, but why.

Conscious Consumerism

When you are about to make a purchase, start by asking yourself: *Do I really need this? Is this aligned with my values? Will I still want this next week?* Mindful spending is about aligning your purchases with what truly matters to you, not what's trending in your social media feed.

Emotional Spending Triggers

We've all been there: bad day, bored at night, mindless scrolling. Next thing you know, your cart has $130 worth of "comfort." Awareness is the first step. Start noticing your patterns:

- Do you shop when you're stressed?

- Are sales your weakness?

- Is the dopamine hit from a new package masking something deeper?

Instead of filling the void with stuff, try a walk, journaling, or calling a friend. Emotional spending is often a temporary fix for a long-term need.

Practicing Gratitude

One of the most underrated financial tools? Gratitude. When you appreciate what you already have, the urge to acquire more fades. Take inventory of the abundance already in your life: your home, your people, your health, your peace. Contentment curbs the craving to consume.

The Minimalist Mindset = Less Spending

Minimalism isn't about having nothing, it's about having only what adds value. The less clutter in your home, the fewer impulse buys you'll make. When you love your space, you're less likely to fill it with things that don't matter.

Money Journaling

Try this: every time you spend, jot it down. Not just the amount—but the *why*.

- "$38 on candles: because I was feeling anxious."

- "$110 on clothes: I wanted to feel better about myself before the event."

This practice creates self-awareness and helps you understand your deeper motivations. Over time, you'll naturally begin to pause before each purchase.

Exercise

To help support this exercise, see the **Mindset Money Journal** in the Appendix Section 6.1.

Chapter 9: Planning for the Long Game

Becoming a mom made me think long-term in a way I never had before. It's not just about making ends meet this month, it's about setting up future-me (and my kids) for stability, freedom, and options.

We often delay thinking about things like retirement, investing, or estate planning because they feel *intimidating* or *distant*. But here's the truth: the earlier you start, even with small amounts, the more power you give your money to grow over time.

I used to believe I'd "figure it out later." But the future comes fast. There's no magical moment when everything aligns perfectly and you suddenly have the time, money, and motivation to start. You just start small. And then you keep going.

Future you, and your family, will be so grateful you did.

401(k)? Don't Leave Free Money on the Table

If your employer offers a 401(k) match, *please* don't ignore it. That's free money. Even if you can't contribute a lot, try to contribute enough to get the full match. Think of it like this: every dollar your employer contributes is a dollar your future self doesn't have to save.

Also, talk to a licensed tax advisor or benefits expert at work. I once learned I wasn't taking full advantage of my company match and had missed out on hundreds of dollars over the years. A 10-minute chat fixed that.

Investing Isn't Just for Rich People

The stock market can feel like a foreign language, but investing doesn't have to be complicated. If you're just starting out, look at:

- **Target-date retirement funds** (based on your expected retirement year)

- **Low-cost index funds** (which track the overall market)

- Apps that round up your spare change into investments (great for dipping your toes in)

You don't need to time the market. You just need to *be in it.*

Life Insurance & Estate Planning (AKA Adulting for Real)

I used to avoid this topic like the plague. But once I had kids, I realized: if something happened to me tomorrow, I want to know my family is okay.

- **Life insurance** is affordable and effective. Even a $500,000 policy can cost less than $30/month.

- **Make a will.** Even if it's simple. Even if you think you don't have "enough" to worry about.

- Add a **medical directive** and **beneficiary designations** for your bank accounts, retirement funds, and insurance. These little things make a big difference when life gets messy.

Set Your 1-Year, 5-Year, and 10-Year Money Goals

This doesn't have to be fancy. But when you write down your goals, you start making decisions that support them. A few examples:

Timeline	Money Goal	Why It Matters
1 Year	Build a $3,000 emergency fund	Peace of mind, fewer credit card emergencies
5 Years	Save for a home down payment	Build equity and stability for my family
10 Years	$100K in retirement savings	Secure financial freedom and early retirement

Revisit these goals every year. Life changes. Your goals can evolve. But don't leave your financial future on autopilot.

Exercise

To help support this exercise, see the **Long Game Goals Worksheet** in the Appendix Section 7.1.

Emma S. Reid

Chapter 10: Gifting on a Budget — Thoughtful, Not Pricey

Being generous doesn't have to mean blowing your budget. With a little planning, creativity, and intention, you can give gifts that feel personal and meaningful, without the last-minute stress or financial strain.

Build a Year-Round Gift Stash

One of the best hacks I swear by is my "gift bin." Tucked away in a closet, it's filled with neutral gifts I've picked up on sale throughout the year with things like:

- Scented candles and cozy socks

- Nice notebooks or journals

- Neutral baby toys or toddler books

- Classic puzzles

I shop for post-holiday clearance and end-of-season sales to stock up, especially for teachers and coworkers. That way, when a birthday or Teacher Appreciation Week sneaks up, I'm ready, and I didn't pay full price.

DIY & Kid-Made = Extra Special

Some of the most cherished gifts aren't bought, they're made. My kids love creating cards for birthdays and holidays. I keep kraft paper rolls on hand so they can decorate our wrapping paper too. Not only is it budget-friendly, but it's a fun bonding activity, and everyone loves a handmade touch.

Budgeting for Gifting (Yes, Add It to the Spreadsheet)

Gifts are a predictable expense, yet so many of us don't actually budget for them. Take a few minutes at the start of the year to list out:

- Family and close friends' birthdays

- Holidays (including Eid, Christmas, Hanukkah, etc.)

- Baby or wedding showers you're anticipating

- Teacher gifts (think: Holidays, End-of-year, Teacher Appreciation Week)

- Graduation season

Estimate how much you *want* to spend, not how much you feel pressured to spend, and set aside a small monthly amount to cover it.

Thoughtful Doesn't Mean Expensive

Some of the most impactful gifts I've given or received cost very little:

- A framed photo of a special memory

- A batch of homemade cookies or bread

- A plant in a cute thrifted pot

- A handwritten letter of appreciation

- A themed "care basket" using Dollar Tree finds

At the end of the day, it's not about how much you spent, it's about the heart behind the gift.

The Great Regifting Debate (Yes, It's Okay!)

My sister and I have *fundamentally different* beliefs on regifting. She sees it as a faux pas, and I see it as a form of thoughtful, intentional giving. And here's the thing: **regifting isn't rude when it's done right.** It's actually one of my favorite low-waste, low-cost ways to pass along something that could genuinely bring someone else joy.

The key? Be thoughtful, not thoughtless.

- **Track who gave it to you** so you don't accidentally give it back to them (or within the same circle).

- Ask yourself: **Would this actually be useful to this person?** Don't regift just to get rid of something.

- Package it up nicely. A pretty bow or handwritten note goes a long way in showing care.

Not only does this save money, but it also helps reduce waste. So many well-intentioned gifts end up gathering dust or going straight to the donation pile. Regifting, when done mindfully, is a form of sustainability, not stinginess.

Exercise

To help support this exercise, see the **Gift Inventory Sheet** in the Appendix Section 8.1.

Emma S. Reid

Chapter 11: Bulk Buying & Stockpiling Smart

Buying in bulk sounds like a no-brainer, until you realize you just spent $70 on snack packs your kids won't touch. The truth? Bulk buying *can* be a brilliant money-saving strategy, but only if it's done with intention and math.

When Bulk Buying Works (and When It Doesn't)

Bulk works best for *non-perishables* and household items you use daily:

- Diapers and wipes

- Toilet paper and paper towels

- Pantry staples (pasta, rice, canned goods)

- Cleaning products

- School snacks

Where can it backfire?

- Produce that spoils quickly

- Trendy items you "might" use

- Anything your family hasn't tried yet (test first in small quantities!)

Unit Price Is Queen

Before tossing that mega box of granola bars in your cart, check the unit price.

- A 24-pack for $14.99 = **$0.62 per bar**

- A 6-pack for $4.99 = **$0.83 per bar**

Multiply that savings over a year and you've got serious cash back in your pocket.

Pro Tip: Keep a note on your phone with "best unit prices" for items you buy often, so you know a real deal when you see one.

Storage That Doesn't Drive You Nuts

Bulk buying can quickly turn into bulk chaos. Avoid clutter and waste with smart storage:

- Use labeled bins or clear containers for snacks and pantry goods.

- Store overflow items (toilet paper, detergent) in closets, under beds, or garage shelves.

- Keep a whiteboard or list of what's in overflow storage so you don't double-buy.

Watch Those Expiration Dates

Don't stockpile like it's the apocalypse. Ask yourself:

- Can I use this up before the expiration?

- Do I have the space to store this?

- Have I bought this before and *actually* used it?

If the answer to any of those is no, skip it—no matter how good the deal sounds.

Smart Stockpile Strategy

Here's what works for many families:

- Keep 1–2 backups of essential household items.

- Rotate your stash: newer in the back, older up front.

- Do a monthly stock check before making your shopping list.

- Buy perishables in bulk *only* if you can prep and freeze portions (like meat, fruits, or bread).

Chapter 12: Home DIY That Won't Break the Bank

You don't need a contractor's license (or a massive renovation budget) to give your space a serious glow-up. Sometimes, it's the smallest upgrades that make the biggest difference, like a fresh coat of paint, new cabinet hardware, or replacing old light switch covers.

Thanks to the magic of the internet, DIY is more accessible than ever. YouTube, Instagram Reels, and TikTok are full of creators showing you step-by-step how to do everything from hanging shelves to flipping furniture, without assuming you already own a full toolbox.

Small Fixes, Big Visual Impact

Here are some budget-friendly upgrades that can totally transform a room:

- Swapping out cabinet knobs and drawer pulls

- Painting an accent wall or your front door

- Adding peel-and-stick backsplash in the kitchen

- Changing light switch covers or outlet plates

- Hanging floating shelves for both function and style

- Re-caulking your tub or sink (easier than it looks!)

Most of these can be done in an afternoon, with minimal tools and supplies.

Starter Tools That Go a Long Way

You don't need a full-blown workshop. Start with these basics:

- Cordless drill (life-changing once you own one)

- Stud finder (for safe and secure hanging)

- Level (no more crooked shelves)

- Caulk gun

- Painter's tape and angled brushes

- Screwdriver set

Buy slowly as you need them. You'll reuse these over and over.

Renter-Friendly DIY

If you're renting, check out these DIY hacks:

- Peel-and-stick wallpaper or backsplash

- Removable hooks and shelves

- Swapping out light fixtures and saving the originals to reinstall later

- Painting (with permission!) in neutral tones

- Rugs, curtains, and lighting can completely change a space without a single hole in the wall

When to DIY vs. Call a Pro

DIY is awesome, *until it's not*. Here's when to call in help:

- Electrical or plumbing work (permits, safety issues)

- Anything involving gas lines or structural changes

- If it involves specialized tools you'd only use once

- You're short on time and precision matters (like tile cutting)

There's no shame in hiring a pro. Sometimes spending to do it right is the most budget-friendly option in the long run.

Exercise

To help support this exercise, see the **DIY Project Planner** in the Appendix Section 9.1.

Chapter 13: Party Planning Without the Price Tag

Let's talk about celebrating, *mindfully*. Whether it's your child's birthday, a baby shower, or a milestone moment, it's easy to fall into the trap of thinking a celebration only counts if it looks like a Pinterest board exploded. But here's the truth: **a meaningful party doesn't have to be expensive**, it just needs intention and a little creativity.

Kids' Birthdays: Cut the Clutter, Keep the Joy

Let's be real, your child won't remember their first few birthdays. I've seen so many well-meaning parents drop $1,000+ on a lavish first birthday: themed balloon arches, luxury bounce houses, and custom cakes. And yes, the Instagram photos are cute. But was it worth it?

Personally, I've thrown **low-cost park parties** for my sons in their early years, and they've been joyful, simple, and memorable for *everyone*. My favorite budget-friendly formula?

- **Time it for breakfast.** Morning parties are cooler during hot days, shorter, and cheaper.

- **Menu:** Coffee for the adults, juice boxes for the kids, bagels, fruit, and some grocery store cupcakes.

- **Cake hack:** Order a plain grocery store cake for under $30 and decorate it yourself with a cute topper or candles.

The kids are happy. The adults are caffeinated. The budget stays intact.

Thoughtful Giving: Ask for What You Actually Need

Another big money (and clutter) saver: **Don't be afraid to guide people on gifts.** One of my favorite birthday requests is:

"Instead of a toy gift, please bring a children's book to add to our home library."

This not only cuts down on the toy pile but builds a meaningful library for your child, and guests love the simplicity.

Showers: Reuse and Reframe

This is my religion: I have **a baby and bridal shower box** filled with decor, signs, cake stands, and random party supplies. Why toss perfectly good decorations when you can reuse them (or lend them to a friend)? This one box has saved me hundreds of dollars over the years.

When it came time for my second baby shower, I knew I wanted to keep things simple, beautiful, and meaningful, without blowing a bunch of money on party favors or games I'd seen (and played) a dozen times.

So I skipped the games entirely. Been there, done that!

Instead, I went to a few local thrift stores and picked up small vases in all shapes and sizes. Then I grabbed some fresh flowers and greenery. We set up a **DIY flower bar** where guests could build their own mini arrangements to take home. It turned into a hands-on activity that everyone loved, and every guest walked away with something special *they* made.

And for my second baby, I skipped the traditional registry altogether. I didn't need more baby gear. What I really needed was diapers and wipes. So the shower turned into a **diaper & wipes sprinkle**, and it was perfect. Friends came, ate good food, made their own flower arrangements, celebrated the baby, and helped us stock up on exactly what we needed. It was low-stress, incredibly helpful, and a great example of how thoughtful planning can be just as impactful as a big budget.

The takeaway? Celebrations don't have to be cookie-cutter or expensive to be meaningful. With a little creativity and intention, you can host something that feels just as joyful without the financial stress.

Quick Budget Party Planning Tips:

- Borrow or reuse decorations and supplies: shop your own house or your friend's!

- Go digital: free invites via text or email save on time and postage.

- Keep food simple: potlucks, brunches, or snacks keep costs (and cleanup) low.

- DIY entertainment: a bubble machine, chalk, or water play at the park is all little ones really need.

The best parties aren't about perfection, they're about connection.

Emma S. Reid

Appendix: Practical Worksheets and Book Club Bonus Content

Appendix Section 1.1: Values Discovery Worksheet

Before you build your values-based budget, take 10 minutes to reflect and write:

1. What brings you joy, peace, or purpose?
Think of small daily moments and big-picture goals.

- _____
- _____
- _____

2. What do you *wish* you had more money for?
Don't limit yourself. Think freely.

- _____
- _____
- _____

3. What are your top 3–5 values?

Circle or list them. Examples:

- Family

- Freedom

- Simplicity

- Travel

- Creativity

- Generosity

- Security

- Health

Your top values with example spending:

- _____

- _____

- _____

4. Where is your current spending not aligned with your values?

Example: Spending $300/month on takeout but wishing you had that for a savings goal or family trip.

- _____

- _____

5. What's one small change you could make this month to better align your spending with your values?

- _____

_____

_____

Appendix Section 1.2: Sample Monthly Budget Template (Values-Based)

Here's a simple framework you can customize. Add or adjust categories as needed.

Category	Budgeted Amount	Notes (Values this supports)
Essentials		
Rent/Mortgage	$	Security
Groceries	$	Health, Family
Insurance (Health, Auto)	$	Peace of mind
Childcare/ Education	$	Family, Future investment
Transportation	$	
Value-Aligned Priorities		

Travel Fund	$	Freedom, Exploration
Weekly Family Outings	$	Connection, Joy
Gym/Yoga Membership	$	Health, Self-care
Creative Tools or Hobbies	$	Creativity
Charitable Giving	$	Generosity
Financial Goals		
Emergency Savings	$	Security
Debt Repayment	$	Freedom
Retirement Contributions	$	Long-term planning

Non-Essentials to Review		
Subscriptions (streaming, etc.)	$	Cancel or consolidate?
Impulse Buys/Fun Shopping	$	Awareness, reduce if not value-based
Takeout/Fast Food	$	Adjust if not intentional

Appendix Section 2.1: Deal Tracker Worksheet

Date	Item/ Service	Source of Deal	Savings

How to Use This Worksheet

1. **Track the date** you found or used a deal.

2. **List the item or service** you purchased (or received for free).

3. **Note the source** (coupon app, marketplace, group, etc.).

4. Record the **original price** and **discounted price** (optional in separate columns).

5. Let the worksheet calculate your **total savings** (you can add formulas if using Excel/Sheets).

6. Use a **notes section** to log promo codes, terms of use, or if it was worth it.

Appendix Section 3.1 Daily Cost Factor Worksheet

Track the small daily expenses that add up over time (weekly, monthly, yearly).

Item / Habit	Freq.	Cost / Time	W	M	Y
Example: Coffee	Daily (5x/week)	$4	$20	$80	$960

Prompts to Reflect:

- What small purchases do I make regularly out of habit?

- Could I enjoy this differently or less often without losing joy?

- Where could these savings go instead?

Appendix Section 3.2 Credit Card Cleanup Worksheet

List out your credit cards to assess which ones to keep, consolidate, or cancel.

Card Name	Balance	Fee	Benefits / Notes
Ex: Chase Sapphire	$0	$95	Great travel rewards, use for flights and hotels

Prompts to Reflect:

- Am I using all the benefits of this card?
- Is the annual fee worth it?
- Do I have more cards than I need?
- Can I consolidate to reduce risk and stay organized?

Appendix Section 4.1: Kids Eat Free Weekly Schedule Worksheet

Track local restaurants and days where kids eat free, so you can plan family meals without breaking the budget!

Day	Restaurant Name	Time / Hours Offered	Notes (Age Limits, Special Offers)
Mon			
Tu			
Wed			
Th			
Fri			
Sat			
Sun			

Tips for Making the Most of "Kids Eat Free" Deals:

- Call ahead to confirm days and times.

- Check if there are minimum adult purchase requirements.

- Look for age restrictions or limits on the number of kids per adult.

- Combine with loyalty programs or coupons for extra savings.

- Take note of special events like "Family Nights" or holiday promotions.

Appendix Section 5.1: Pantry Inventory Tracker

Fill this out regularly to keep track of what you have, plan meals around those items, and reduce waste.

Item Name	Qty	Exp. Date	Notes (e.g., needs to be used soon, good for soups, etc.)

Appendix Section 6.1: Money Mindset Journal Template

Use this template to reflect on your spending habits, emotional triggers, and moments of gratitude. Aim to fill this out daily or weekly for the best insights.

Date	Purchase	$	Why did I buy it?	How do I feel about it now?
MM/DD	e.g. Candle	$18	Felt stressed after work	Still glad I bought it, it helps me relax
MM/DD	e.g. Takeout	$26	Too tired to cook	Would have saved if I meal prepped

Reflection Prompts (Use weekly or monthly)

- What spending patterns am I noticing?

- Which purchases brought me the most joy or value?

- Which ones do I regret, and why?

- What emotional states led to the most spending?

- How can I handle those emotions differently next time?

- What am I grateful for that doesn't cost anything?

Appendix Section 7.1: Long Game Goals Worksheet

Time line	Money Goal	Why It Matters	How Much I Need	Steps to Start
1 Y	Save $3,000 for emergency	To feel secure if costs come up	$3K	Auto-transfer $250/ month into savings
5 Y	Down payment on a house	Create a stable home for my family	$30K	Start a savings account
10 Y	$100K in retirement funds	Long-term indep.	$100K	Max out Roth IRA yearly

How to Use:

- **Money Goal**: Be specific (e.g., "Emergency fund," "Roth IRA contributions," "Kids' college fund")

- **Why This Matters**: Motivation lives here. Remind yourself *why* you're doing this.

- **Target Amount**: What you're aiming to save or invest

Appendix Section 8.1: Gift Inventory Sheet

Item	Occasion(s)	Qty	Notes (Where Bought, Price, etc.)
Scented candle	Teacher gift, Birthday	3	Target clearance - $3 each
Wooden baby toy	Baby Shower	2	Amazon BOGO deal
Hardcover journal	Birthday, Thank You	4	Marshalls - $5 each
Kids' sticker books	Birthday	5	Dollar Tree - $1.25 each
Cozy socks	Holidays, Self-care	3	Old Navy sale - $2 each

DIY bath salt jars	Holiday, Teacher	6	Made at home, total cost $10

Pro tip: Add extra columns for "Given To" if you want to keep track of who you've gifted each item to, to avoid duplicates next year, and "Category" and "Age Range" if you want to be more specific with your tracking.

Appendix Section 9.1: DIY Project Planner

Project Name:

_____

Room/Space:

_____

Goal/Outcome:
- ☐ Refresh the look
- ☐ Add storage
- ☐ Improve function
- ☐ Repurpose old item
- ☐ Other:

_____

Notes:

_____

_____

Supplies + Tools Needed

Item	Have It? Y/N	Need to Buy? Y/N	Estimated Cost

Total Estimated Budget: $_____

Appendix Section 10.1: Book Club Bonus Content

1. Discussion Questions

Money Mindset:

- What beliefs about money did you grow up with, and how have they changed?

- How do you define "financial freedom" for yourself?

- What's one limiting money belief you want to release?

Spending with Intention:

- What does "value-based spending" look like in your life right now?

- Have you ever regretted saving too much or spending too little?

- What's a recent expense that brought you genuine joy?

Mental Health:

- How does money stress show up in your life?

- What's helped you manage financial anxiety?

Building Wealth:

- What does wealth mean beyond money?

- Are you investing in your future self today? How?

- How can we support each other as a group on our financial goals?

2. Money Intentions Worksheet (Group or Solo Use)

Prompt Ideas:

- In 1 year, I want to feel _____ about my finances.

- The money habit I most want to build is _____.

- I am currently avoiding _____ and it's time to face it with compassion.

- One small action I'll take this week: _____.

3. Mindful Money Practices (Book Club Activity)

Try a short grounding or action step together:

- 2-minute "future self" visualization

- Silent journaling: "What would calm, confident me do next with my money?"

- Mini financial audit: review one category and ask, "Is this aligned with my values?"

- Share a "money win" from the past month, big or small

4. Wrap-Up Reflection:

- Favorite aha moment from the book?

- What's one belief or habit that's shifted for you?

- What's next on your financial journey?

5. Bonus Book Club Email Template or Invite Text

Example:

> *Hey friends! I'm starting a book club to read* **The Money Mindful Millennial**—*a smart, shame-free guide to building a better relationship with money. We'll talk about money mindsets, mindful spending, and financial freedom without the pressure. Want to join?*

About the Author

Emma S. Reid is a millennial mom, deal hunter, and lifelong learner who believes that financial empowerment starts with the everyday choices we make. With a passion for budgeting, secondhand finds, and turning chaos into calm, she shares real-life strategies to help others live well for less.

When she's not writing or hunting for bargains, she's raising her family, trying out a new DIY project, or reorganizing her pantry just for fun.

If you enjoyed this book, please leave a review on Amazon!

www.ingramcontent.com/pod-product-compliance
Lightning Source LLC
Chambersburg PA
CBHW031220120626
46545CB00003B/925